Yellow Light

for Mark,
the better fiction,
from Garrett with
admiration & love

26 Dec. '84
Nashville

The Wesleyan Poetry Program : Volume 104

YELLOW
LIGHT

poems by
Garrett Kaoru Hongo

 WESLEYAN UNIVERSITY PRESS
Middletown, Connecticut

I am grateful to the Thomas J. Watson Foundation of Providence, Rhode Island, for a travel grant that enabled me to live in Japan and have the experience out of which several of these poems come.

Certain poems in this collection were included in a manuscript which was awarded First Prize in the Major Poetry Division of the Avery and Jule Hopwood Creative Writing Contests at The University of Michigan in 1975.

My special thanks to Mark Lundsten, Greg Pape, and Lance Patigian—*sennin no kai.*

Original publication of poems in this book: *Amerasia Journal,* "Kubota" under the title "Kubota Walks Out"; *Antaeus,* "Who Among You Knows the Essence of Garlic?"; *Bachy,* "Stay with Me"; *Bamboo Ridge,* "C & H Sugar Strike, Kahuku, 1923"; *The Blaisdell Journal,* "To Matsuo Basho and Kawai Sora in Nirvana"; *Greenfield Review,* "Roots"; *Harvard Magazine,* "Something Whispered in the *Shakuhachi*"; *Hawaii Review,* "The Hongo Store" and "What For"; *Iron Country,* "Postcards for Bert Meyers"; *The Journal of Ethnic Studies,* "And Your Soul Shall Dance"; *Kayak,* "Off from Swing Swift" and "Preaching the Blues"; *Missouri Review,* "On the Last Performance of *Musumé Dojoji* at the Nippon-Kan of the Astor Hotel, Seattle, Washington"; *Momentum,* "Issei: First-Generation Japanese American"; *The Nation,* Section 1 from "Stepchild" under the title "Evacuation"; *The New Yorker,* "Yellow Light"; *Poetry Northwest,* "A Restless Night"; *The Reaper,* "Dream of a Trumpet"; *Seattle Review,* "Winnings." "Cruising 99" was published as a section of the anthology *The Buddha Bandits Down Highway 99* (1978).

Grateful acknowledgment is made to Harcourt Brace Jovanovich, Inc. for permission to reprint and adapt excerpts from *America Is in the Heart* by Carlos Bulosan, copyright © 1943, 1946 by Harcourt, Brace and Company, Inc.

The selections from testimonies by Tokio Akagi and Paul Chikamasa Horiuchi are derived from *Issei: A History of Japanese Immigrants in North America,* edited by Kazuo Ito and translated by Shinichiro Nakamura and Jean S. Gerard, published by The Executive Committee for Publication (Seattle, Japanese Community Service), copyright © 1973 by Kazuo Ito.

Library of Congress Cataloging in Publication Data

Hongo, Garrett Kaoru, 1951–
    Yellow light.

    ([The Wesleyan poetry program; v. 104])
    I. Title. II. Series.
PS3558.048Y4   811'.54   81-16050
ISBN 0-8195-2104-3   AACR2
ISBN 0-8195-1104-8 (pbk.)

Manufactured in the United States of America   First edition for Cynthia

Contents

Yellow Light

One arm hooked around the frayed strap
of a tar-black patent-leather purse,
the other cradling something for dinner:
fresh bunches of spinach from a J-Town *yaoya,*
sides of split Spanish mackerel from Alviso's,
maybe a loaf of Langendorf; she steps
off the hissing bus at Olympic and Fig,
begins the three-block climb up the hill,
passing gangs of schoolboys playing war,
Japs against Japs, Chicanas chalking sidewalks
with the holy double-yoked crosses of hopscotch,
and the Korean grocer's wife out for a stroll
around this neighborhood of Hawaiian apartments
just starting to steam with cooking
and the anger of young couples coming home
from work, yelling at kids, flicking on
TV sets for the Wednesday Night Fights.

If it were May, hydrangeas and jacaranda
flowers in the streetside trees would be
blooming through the smog of late spring.
Wisteria in Masuda's front yard would be
shaking out the long tresses of its purple hair.
Maybe mosquitoes, moths, a few orange butterflies
settling on the lattice of monkey flowers
tangled in chain-link fences by the trash.

But this is October, and Los Angeles
seethes like a billboard under twilight.

From used-car lots and the movie houses uptown,
long silver sticks of light probe the sky.
From the Miracle Mile, whole freeways away,
a brilliant fluorescence breaks out
and makes war with the dim squares
of yellow kitchen light winking on
in all the side streets of the Barrio.

She climbs up the two flights of flagstone
stairs to 201-B, the spikes of her high heels
clicking like kitchen knives on a cutting board,
props the groceries against the door,
fishes through memo pads, a compact,
empty packs of chewing gum, and finds her keys.

The moon then, cruising from behind
a screen of eucalyptus across the street,
covers everything, everything in sight,
in a heavy light like yellow onions.

Off from Swing Shift

Late, just past midnight,
freeway noise from the Harbor
and San Diego leaking in
from the vent over the stove,
and he's off from swing shift at Lear's.
Eight hours of twisting circuitry,
charting ohms and maximum gains
while transformers hum
and helicopters swirl
on the roofs above the small factory.
He hails me with a head-fake,
then the bob and weave
of a weekend middleweight
learned at the Y on Kapiolani
ten years before I was born.

The shoes and gold London Fogger
come off first, then the easy grin
saying he's lucky as they come.
He gets into the slippers
my brother gives him every Christmas,
carries his Thermos over to the sink,
and slides into the one chair at the table
that's made of wood and not yellow plastic.
He pushes aside stacks
of *Sporting News* and *Outdoor Life,*
big round tins of Holland butter cookies,
and clears a space for his elbows, his pens,
and the *Racing Form*'s Late Evening Final.

His left hand reaches out,
flicks on the Sony transistor
we bought for his birthday
when I was fifteen.
The right ferries in the earphone,
a small, flesh-colored star,
like a tiny miracle of hearing,
and fits it into place.
I see him plot black constellations
of figures and calculations
on the magazine's margins,
alternately squint and frown
as he fingers the knob of the tuner
searching for the one band
that will call out today's results.

There are whole cosmologies
in a single handicap,
a lifetime of two-dollar losing
in one pick of the Daily Double.

Maybe tonight is his night
for winning, his night
for beating the odds
of going deaf from a shell
at Anzio still echoing
in the cave of his inner ear,
his night for cashing in
the blue chips of shrapnel still grinding
at the thickening joints of his legs.

But no one calls
the horse's name, no one
says Shackles, Rebate, or Pouring Rain.
No one speaks a word.

He's always there, waiting for me
to step off the plane, swing
the rubble of my luggage
from my gambler's hands
over to his own, bruised and blue
as his music. He's dressed
in faded denims and the flower prints
of a sailcloth aloha shirt, furling
in the blast of fanjets and Santana wind.

I'm home because Seattle quit on me,
because my hands went soft
drawing straights and busted flushes,
because I couldn't make it outside,
and I'm coming in, calling out
the changes of an old tune.

Outside, 747s scream over runways,
tuck the talons of their landing gear
into gleaming bellies, fat with baggage.
Los Angeles generates its neon—
flashcubes of office lights going off
at TRW and Northrup Electric.

We run the give-and-go, pick-
and-roll through the parking lot,
tossing a ring of keys
like a basketball, drive the lane
to his big blue van, swing
into the cab, and slam the doors
on the rest of the free world.

"Big El," I say. "Hey, Mouth Harp,"
he calls back, and we shoot out
over Century, through the on-ramp,
and onto the speed lane of the San Diego.

He hums an old blues, bad
and niggerbold, any old way
you want, tells me Dad's
legs are worse, Mom's still
working Pedro on Saturdays
and Tuesday nights, that he's
still shoveling two weeks of shit
in the pile between paychecks.

When we were younger, unscarred
and still reaching out for other names,
he would be in the garage
with his guitar, an amplifier
the size of a shoe box, practicing
for the priesthood, preaching the blues.

The freezer hummed,
axles on the Plymouth
wept, sketching a calligraphy
of quarter tones, staffs, and scales
in the notes of a new gospel
hymning from his hands.

He was only fourteen, dressed
in street rhymes and a borrowed
chamois jacket, the coming scars
shining in harmonies of light
from the floor's black oil.

The off-ramp comes quickly, swerves
us past Volvo, Toyota, Nissan,
Marietta Aluminum, and the big
trucking lot that owns my name.

Gardena's Nisei bars, *okazuyas*,
and liquor stores are all closed,
the nurseries have put on
their caftans of cotton sheets,
their robes of pearlescent silk
gleaming over azaleas and dwarf pines.

There is no noise, no noise
at all—none but the throb
in my brother's throat, swelling
with blues, and stoplights
in all the streets chanting Go,
Slow, and No Go to the night.

Stay with Me

At six o'clock, most people
already sitting down to dinner
and the Evening News, Gloria's
still on the bus, crying
in a back seat, her face
bathed in soft blue light
from the fluorescent lamps.
She leans her head down
close to her knees, tugs
at the cowl of her raincoat
so it covers her eyes, tries
to mask her face and stifle
the sobbing so the young black
in the seat across the aisle
won't notice her above the
disco music pouring from
his radio and filling the bus.
He does anyway, and, curious,
bends towards her, placing a hand
on her shoulder, gently,
as if consoling a child
after the first disappointment,
asking, "Is it cool, baby?"

She nods, and, reassured,
he starts back to his seat,
but she stops him, sliding
her hand over his, wanting
to stroke it, tapping it instead,
rhythmically, as if his hand
were a baby's back and she
its mother, singing and rocking
it softly to sleep. The black
wishes he could jerk his hand

away, say something hip to save
himself from all that's not
his business, something like
"Get back, Mama! You a fool!"
but he can't because Gloria's
just tucked her chin over
both their hands, still resting
on her shoulder, clasped them
on the ridge of her jaw the way
a violinist would hold a violin.

He can feel the loose skin
around her neck, the hard bone
of her jaw, the pulse
in her throat thudding against
his knuckles, and still he wants
to pull away, but hesitates,
stammers, asks again,
"Hey . . . Is it okay?"

He feels something hot
hit his arm, and, too late
to be startled now, sighs
and gives in, turning his
hand over, lifting it, clasping
hers, letting her bring it
to her cheek, white and slick
with tears, stroking her face
with the back of his hand,
rubbing the hollow of her cheek
against his fist, and she,
speaking finally, "Stay with me
a little while. Till your stop?
Just stay with me," as her face
blooms and his shines
in the blue fluorescent light.

Winnings

It's Gardena, late Saturday afternoon
on Vermont Avenue, near closing time
at the thrift store, and my father's
left me to rummage through trash bins
stuffed with used paperbacks, 25¢ a pound,
while he chases down some bets
at the card clubs across the street.

The register rings up its sales—$2.95,
$11.24, $26.48 for the reclaimed Frigidaire—
and a girl, maybe six or so, barefoot,
in a plaid dress, her hair braided
in tight cornrows, tugs at the strap
of her mother's purse, begging a few
nickels for the gumball machine.

She skips through the check-stand,
runs toward the electric exit, passing
a fleet of shopping carts, bundles
of used-up magazines (*Ebony* and *Jet*)
stacked in pyramids in the far aisle,
reaches the bright globe of the vendor,
fumbles for her coins, and works the knob.

My father comes in from the Rainbow
across the street, ten hands of Jacks
or Better, five draw, a winner
with a few dollars to peel away
from grocery money and money to fix
the washer, a dollar for me to by
four pounds of Pocket Wisdoms, Bantams,

a Dell that says *Walt Whitman, Poet
of the Open Road*, and hands it to me,
saying "We won, *Boy-san*! We Won!"
as the final blast of sunset kicks through
plate glass and stained air, firing through
the thicket of neon across the street,
consuming the store, the girl, the dollar bill,

even the Rainbow and the falling night
in a brief symphony of candied light.

What For

At six I lived for spells:
how a few Hawaiian words could call
up the rain, could hymn like the sea
in the long swirl of chambers
curling in the nautilus of a shell,
how Amida's ballads of the Buddhaland
in the drone of the priest's liturgy
could conjure money from the poor
and give them nothing but mantras,
the strange syllables that healed desire.

I lived for stories about the war
my grandfather told over *hana* cards,
slapping them down on the mats
with a sharp Japanese *kiai*.

I lived for songs my grandmother sang
stirring curry into a thick stew,
weaving a calligraphy of Kannon's love
into grass mats and straw sandals.

I lived for the red volcano dirt
staining my toes, the salt residue
of surf and sea wind in my hair,
the arc of a flat stone skipping
in the hollow trough of a wave.

I lived a child's world, waited
for my father to drag himself home,
dusted with blasts of sand, powdered rock,
and the strange ash of raw cement,
his deafness made worse by the clang
of pneumatic drills, sore in his bones
from the buckings of a jackhammer.

He'd hand me a scarred lunchpail,
let me unlace the hightop G.I. boots,
call him the new name I'd invented
that day in school, write it for him
on his newspaper. He'd rub my face
with hands that felt like gravel roads,
tell me to move, go play, and then he'd
walk to the laundry sink to scrub,
rinse the dirt of his long day
from a face brown and grained as koa wood.

I wanted to take away the pain
in his legs, the swelling in his joints,
give him back his hearing,
clear and rare as crystal chimes,
the fins of glass that wrinkled
and sparked the air with their sound.

I wanted to heal the sores that work
and war had sent to him,
let him play catch in the backyard
with me, tossing a tennis ball
past papaya trees without the shoulders
of pain shrugging back his arms.

I wanted to become a doctor of pure magic,
to string a necklace of sweet words
fragrant as pine needles and plumeria,
fragrant as the bread my mother baked,
place it like a lei of cowrie shells
and *pikake* flowers around my father's neck,
and chant him a blessing, a sutra.

Cruising 99

for Lawson Fusao Inada and Alan Chong Lau

I.

A PORPHYRY OF ELEMENTS

Starting in a long swale between the Sierras
    and the Coast Range,
Starting from ancient tidepools of a Pleistocene sea,
Starting from exposed granite bedrock,
From sandstone and shale, glaciated, river-worn,
    and scuffed by wind,
Tired of the extremes of temperature,
    the weather's wantonness,
Starting from the survey of a condor's eye
Cutting circles in the sky over Tehachapi and Tejon,
Starting from lava flow and snow on Shasta,
    a head of white hair,
    a garland of tongue-shaped obsidian,
Starting from the death of the last grizzly,
The final conversion of Tulare County
    to the internal-combustion engine,
Starting from California oak and acorn,
    scrubgrass, rivermist,
    and lupine in the foothills,
From days driving through the outfield clover
    of Modesto in a borrowed Buick,
From nights drinking pitchers of dark
    in the Neon Moon Bar & Grill,
From mornings grabbing a lunchpail, work gloves,
    and a pisspot hat,
From Digger pine and Douglas fir and aspen around Placerville,
From snowmelt streams slithering into the San Joaquin,
From the deltas and levees and floods of the Sacramento,
From fall runs of shad, steelhead, and salmon,

From a gathering of sand, rock, gypsum, clay,
  limestone, water, and tar,
From a need or desire to throw your money away
  in The Big City,
From a melting of history and space in the crucible
  of an oil-stained hand—
Starting from all of these, this porphyry of elements,
  this aggregate of experiences
Fused like feldspar and quartz to the azure stone
  of memory and vision,
Starting from all of these and an affectionate eye
  for straight, unending lines,
We hit this old road of Highway Ninety-Nine!

II.

A SAMBA FOR INADA

Let's go camping
Let's go chanting
Let's go cruising
Let's go boozing

Let's go smoke
Let's go folk
Let's go rock
Let's go bop

Let's go jazz
Let's go fast
Let's go slow
Let's go blow

Let's go Latin
Let's go cattin
Let's go jiving
Let's go hiding

Let's go disco
Let's go Frisco
Let's go blues
Let's go cruise

Let's go far
Let's go near
Let's go camping
Let's go chanting

Let's go lazy
Let's go boozing
Let's go crazy
Let's go cruising

III.

CRUISING IN THE GREATER VEHICLE / A JAM SESSION

"Well, goddamnit, Lawson! Whyn't you play in key and keep to the rhythm? First you say you wanna go back to Fresno, back to the fish store and Kamaboko Gardens on the West Side, and then you say, forget it, I take it back, let's go to the Sacto *Bon-Odori* instead."

"Yeah. And this ain't even *shoyu* season yet, chump!"

"Awww, hell. What's wrong with you two? Can't you improvise? You know, I'm just laying down a bass, man. Just a rhythm, a scale, something to jam on, something to change, find our range, something to get us going. Once we get started, we can work our way around to Weed, put on some tire chains, or break down in Selma, refuse to buy grapes, raisins, or Gallo, do a pit-stop at a Sacto sporting goods, pick up some air mattresses shaped like pearl-diving women, and float all day downriver to the deltas, sipping Cokes and *saké* in the summer heat."

"Shit. Whyn't you just solo and forget the rest of us? You start chanting and pretty soon we're hearing the entire Lotus Sutra."

"You two Buddhaheads just a pair of one-eyed Japs with dishpan hands and deadpan minds, man. This is the Champ Chonk talking, and we're playing Chinese anaconda. Eight-card, no-peek or *pak-kai*, roll your own, hi-lo, three for sweep, four for hot-sour soup stud, and neither of you's put down your ante yet. So shit or get off the *shu-mai*, fellas."

"Calm down and watch the road, Alan."

"Who's driving this heap, anyway?"

"I thought you were."

"I thought Lawson was."

"Don't worry. This is a dodo-driven, autopiloted, cruise-controlled, Triple-A-mapped, Flying-A-gassed, dual-overhead-cam, Super-Sofistifunktified, Frijole Guacamole, Gardena Guahuanco, Chonk Chalupa Cruiser with Buddha Bandit Bumpers, Jack!"

"Where we going, Alan?"

"Where do you think? We're going to Paradise."

IV.

ON THE ROAD TO PARADISE

Distances don't matter
nor the roll of the road past walnut groves.
It's sky that counts,
the color of it at dawn or sunset,
a match more true to the peach
than a mix of oils by Matisse.
Or maybe it's actually weather
we love most, the way it shifts
and scatters over the state
like radio waves bouncing off the face of the moon.

The one over there, near Yuba City,
rising over a backyard garden
of onions, tomatoes, squash, and corn.
The one with the spider
scrambling through celery,
harvesting moths and mayflies
from the web it has strung between stalks.
Sometimes I wish I could harvest the weather,
reap it like wheat or rice,
store it in a silo
announcing STEADY RAIN or CLEAR SKIES on its sides.
When the prices rise,
I could ship hailstorms or Santanas in orange crates,
make Safeway go broke,
do something politically efficacious for a change.
But all I really do besides write these poems
is allow my mind to wander while I drive.
There it goes, down the arroyo,
through manzanita and Mormon tea.
Or there, up the mustard and Indian pipe on the hill.
Might as well let it.
Nothing but God and Country on the radio now.
Wolfman Jack's syndicated and the Dodgers
haven't made it to Vero Beach.
I wish this road would turn or bend,
intersect with a spy movie, some Spanish galleon,
or maybe a Chinese poem with landscapes
in brocade, mist, wine, and moonlight.
This California moon is yellow most of the time,
like it was stained with nicotine,
or sealed in amber like an insect.
Why is it always better somewhere else?
Why do I always wish I were Tu Fu?

V.

PALMISTRY FANTASIA

There, the pasteboard and neon hand!
Just past the interchange by the bowling alley.
The one with silver rockets, small green stars,
and a trail of red comets flashing through the smog.

It's still here, the hand
held up in greeting or command.
"Halt!" it says, or
"Peace be with you, brother,"
while the map across its palm
traces excursions into blue trees,
green skies, and mushroom-colored lives.

Blue dun is the color of its neon,
the same as the throat feathers of a teal
scudding over the marshes of Merced.
It matches the purple mascara the gypsy woman wears,
matches the pools of velvet-blue darkness in her eyes.

Her name is Alma Josephina,
and she designed the sign herself,
imitating the figure of her own hand,
the neon indicative of its natural aura.

That was twenty years ago
when Eisenhower was President
and all her customers wore pedal pushers
or Bermudas, and never noticed
the fireflies in the marshes at night.

*

You're Oriental, aren't you?
Can you read tea leaves?
I tried to once, years ago,
had a Chinese woman teaching me,
but her fees were too steep.

I like a joke.
It loosens up the customers.

Well, come here towards the light.
Let me get a good look
at the ghosts in the grave of your palm.
They're there, you know.
All the people you've even been,
all the trips you've taken
and towns you've settled in,
back before the birth of Christ,
back before people were people,
before this paw was a hand.

You see? The whole palm glows
like purple mist over a cemetery.
Move closer. Clamp it around the glass.
See it flare on the inside?
That's the light your bones make,
not the crystal at all.

Look at your hand now.
You can see yourself dancing
on the heel just above the wrist.
You must be a happy man.
You'll be born again and again,
get to the threshold of Heaven,
never enter but keep coming back,

here, for fun, for friends,
until this will be Paradise,
and Paradise just an old resort
the highway's passed by.

Well, have a nice trip.
You'll make it yet.
Says so right in that curvy line
around the Mound of Venus,
that thumbstump there,
right where the long straight line
cuts across like an interstate.

VI.

POSTCARDS SENT HOME

1.

Dust rolls out of the hills like fog,
and it's too hot for shoes or shirts.
I'd like to take my hair off too,
peel it from my head, dip it in a bucket of ice,
and wear it around my neck like a bandana.

2.

Crickets attend the night,
add a falsetto drone
to the sound of us
pissing in tumbleweeds.

3.

There's a Tastee-Freeze in Fresno,
the A & Dub's closed down,
Jack-in-the-Box keeps popping up,
and McDonald's owns the town.

4.

Somebody's drying tobacco leaves
on the laundry line.
There, see them furl
and flap next to the nylons?

5.

A giant oak uncurls over the road,
sprinkles a fine yellow powder on the windshield.
The sun hits, touches it off
in a spasm of golden-red light.

VII.

BODY & FENDER / BODY & SOUL

At the grill, the Indian girl with buckteeth and dimples serves us a round
of coffee and sweet rolls. We're waiting for the guy at Henley's Texaco,
down the street, to find us a fan belt that'll fit. It's early, the sky's still in
the john, shaving, and the sports page has to wait to get in. Everybody's
grumpy. We sit around, jab at raisins with our forks, and try to look as
tough as the waitress.

Her name's Rita. Her brothers jump fires and pump
oil in Alaska. Her sisters string beads and make babies back on the Res.
Her ex is white, a logger who threatened never to come back and didn't.
She doesn't hold any grudges. That's why she's so nice, why she pops her
gum filling the salt and pepper shakers, why she adjusts her girdle so we
can see, why the egg spot on her dress doesn't show.

Outside, the sun eases up over
the parking lot, scrambles across the freeway, and runs for cover behind a
pile of pumpkin-colored clouds. 99 starts shuffling its deck of cars and
pickups, getting set to deal a hand of nine-to-five stud. We don't watch.
This is Redding, and ain't nothing thing going on besides the day shift.

Alan says, "Look, there's Venus," and
points to a piece of light draining into the sky. I want to order a country-
fried steak, talk about the Dodgers, but there isn't time. Lawson hums a
few chords, stirring the changes with his coffee spoon.

Rita cruises back like
a bus bound for Reno, starts dealing some ashtrays. She says, "How's it
going, boys?"

I answer for all of us—"Hey, Rita. It's almost gone."

VIII.

PILGRIMAGE TO THE SHRINE

Six hours since
the Paradise Cutoff
and running on empty.
No gas stations or rest stops,
no weigh stations, no cops.
Just miles of straight road
and a long double-yellow
unrolling in front of us.

Alan recognizes nothing.
Lawson pops the glove,
pulls out a penlight,
and fingers the map,
pronouncing a few mantras.

Our headlights slide
over a scarecrow
made of tumbleweeds
standing by the road.

He's wearing a *kimono*,
a dark-blue stovepipe hat,
his shoulders cloaked
in a wreath of chrysanthemums.

We pull over,
back up,
and he disappears
into the pale-
grey darkness.

It's smoke.
We can smell it,
so somebody's
got to be
close by.

But our eyes
go blind, fill
with tears and ashes
as we stumble
down the off-ramp.

The smell of
frying trout
and steamed rice
reaches us when
we come to.

An old hermit,
dressed like the scarecrow,
crawls out of his barracks
and brings us tea.

"Drink!" he says,
"It'll pick you up!"
And so we drink,
feeling drugged.

Soft blues
in the key
of sleep
suffocates the air.

From up the mountain,
the sound of obsidian,
flaking in the wind.
Clouds of black glass
waltz around us.

We dress ourselves
in shrouds of tule reeds
stitched with barbed wire,
stained with salt and mud.

We refuse to cry.

We drift back
to the highway,
holding our fists
like rattles,
shaking them
like bones.

IX.

CONFESSION OF THE HIGHWAY/THE HERMIT SPEAKS

I know the rituals, the spells of grapes,
the ceremonies of tomatoes, celery, and rice.
I know the color of wind dressed for fiesta,
and the names of carnivals in Spanish and Japanese.
I am familiar with the determination of *campesinos*
who migrate up and down the stretch of the state
in search of crops ready for harvest.
It's all a dull ache in my back,
small cuts on the throats of my fingers,
and the alkali of a dry lake in my lungs.
For me, the oracle of the giant orange
always predicts good fortune,
yet, it never comes true.
My stomach is full of sand and tar,
a little bit of paint, a few crickets.
I stand in swampwater up to my hips,
and the stink of rotting figs
escapes from my armpits in small brown clouds.
Scrub oak and tumbleweed sprout from my scalp,
make a small grove behind my left ear.
I don't know why sparrows and starlings
refuse to approach me, to take the grass seed
tucked in the cuffs of my trousers.
Maybe it's the stain of asphalt around my ankles,
this copper sheen of sweat on my back.
Sometimes, when the valley heat
makes the bones in my feet
start to hiss and burn,
the desire to escape comes over me again.
I can't help it.
My arms pull down a few telephone posts,
my shoulders churn against the bindings.
I feel myself wanting to sit up,

begin to walk again, and thresh my way
across rice fields and acres of alfalfa.
For once I'd like to lift my face
straight above Shasta into the sky,
shout in unison with thunder,
roar with the assurance of Santana wind,
leap out of these bonds of copper and steel,
slough off this skin of cement,
and walk south or north or even west
into the weather and the sea.

Postcards for Bert Meyers

I.

Y<small>AMANOTE</small> S<small>EN</small>

The Cliffside Line

Steel rails gleam with fatigued light.
Cement grows its age spots of tobacco and gum.
A vendor chants his selling call—
Bento! Bento!—louder than a curse,
Older than literature. Bells clang

And the conductor shrieks on his whistle,
Shoves another body through the buzzing doors,
Flaps the slender wedge of his red flag,
And disappears down the arcade of yellow faces.

Air brakes hiss like spitting cats.
Posters streak into montage.
Someone blows his nose and doors close,
Finds a corner and squeezes into his newspaper.

Salary men bump into breasts and bras,
Lock arms around a briefcase and hope.
Everywhere people bob and stagger
As if standing in the surf.

At the next stop we slide—
And finally hear ourselves talk,
As the train breathes again
And lets out a small puff
Full of tiny Japanese people.

II.

MIDNIGHT IN TOKYO

My tea turns cold in the Sierra cup.
The taste of metal on my tongue.
I draw figure eights, infinity signs,
On a newspaper I cannot read,
And ash my smoke in a junkpile of butts.

In the streets below,
Where flyers and torn bits of leaves
Toss and tumble in their sleep,
A cat's wail evaporates into silence.

Across the way, on the apartment-house roof,
A week's load of pink and blue panties
Hang on the knuckles of a bamboo pole,
Suspended by their translucent crotches.

A rushing sound comes up from the station.
Then the muffled racketing of the train
Carries through the still night air.
The city mumbles from a dream,
Calling an old lover back to bed.

III.

AUBADE, LATE FALL

after Shiki

The trolley skates along an empty street.
Owls glide over grey tile roofs
On and on towards the mountains,
Straight into the dawn.

Frost pumps its mist from the ground,
And the sun slants through the fence's
Bamboo frame, scatters light like rice
Over a graveyard of Buddhas.

A bell booms deeper than silence,
And a ragpicker crawls from his cardboard hut,
Walks up the temple steps, stops
By the trash, rummages for a cigarette.

IV.

ALONE IN A SHOWER

Drizzling, and the street secretes
its car grease, beading on asphalt.
I duck under the canvas awning
of a coffeehouse, and the air

inflates like a sponge around me.
The trolley car stopped in its slot
seals itself again and becomes
a terrarium for plants in sweaters

and topcoats. One, tilting and
cramped for space, presses a leaf
against the window glass,
flat and splayed as a palm

would be. The billiard parlor
across the way douses its neon
and fades into grey. A taxi
splashes by on its rubber skates,

brown roostertails of mud spuming
over the street. All around me
the ten thousand things
of the universe go slack

in the day's new lagoon,
and I seep out of myself like
water from the soaked earth,
like rain from the black sky.

V.

FROM AN INN AT ATAMI

Boots stowed on a shelf downstairs,
socks hang like hand puppets
from hooks on a wall
the same shade of blue
as Levi's or lapis lazuli.

Outside, the sun hunches down
behind a screen of cypresses,
casts a net of shadows
over the bay, its surface stippled
by fish rising to feed.
On the horizon, an airplane
buzzes like a power saw,
a black X over the sea.
Some kind of animal,
maybe a monkey or crow,
chatters in the bamboo grove below.

Tomorrow to Ise,
to the shrines where my family
has not made pilgrimage
for more than a hundred years.
I'll toss a copper *yen*-piece,
clap twice and bow,
call on the land's most terrible god
to give us back our name.

Who Among You Knows the Essence of Garlic?

Can your foreigner's nose smell mullets
roasting in a glaze of brown bean paste
and sprinkled with novas of sea salt?

Can you hear my grandmother
chant the mushroom's sutra?

Can you hear the papayas crying
as they bleed in porcelain plates?

I'm telling you that the bamboo
slips the long pliant shoots
of its myriad soft tongues
into your mouth that is full of oranges.

I'm saying that the silver waterfalls
of bean threads will burst in hot oil
and stain your lips like zinc.

The marbled skin of the blue mackerel
works good for men. The purple oils
from its flesh perfume the tongues of women.

If you swallow them whole, the rice cakes
soaking in a broth of coconut milk and brown sugar
will never leave the bottom of your stomach.

Flukes of giant black mushrooms
leap from their murky tubs
and strangle the toes of young carrots.

Broiling chickens ooze grease,
yellow tears of fat collect
and spatter in the smoking pot.

Soft ripe pears, blushing
on the kitchen window sill,
kneel like plump women
taking a long, luxurious shampoo,
and invite you to bite their hips.

Why not grab basketfuls of steaming noodles,
lush and slick as the hair of a fine lady,
and squeeze?

The shrimps, big as Portuguese thumbs,
stew among cut guavas, red onions,
ginger root, and rosemary in lemon juice,
the palm oil bubbling to the top,
breaking through layers and layers
of shredded coconut and sliced cashews.

Who among you knows the essence
of garlic and black lotus root,
of red and green peppers sizzling
among squads of oysters in the skillet,
of crushed ginger, fresh green onions,
and pale-blue rice wine simmering
in the stomach of a big red fish?

To Matsuo Basho and Kawai Sora in Nirvana

I wanted to walk
on the shore of Matsushima,
maybe write a hip *haiku*
where Basho saw smiling frogs
hump croaking ones.

He and Sora hired a boat,
put down on Ojima Beach,
crossing over from the south
around about noon or so,
mending a *momohiki* or two.
Maybe they squatted
among pines or cherry trees
and let the wind
billow their robes,
composing poems on a cloud
while the surf sighed
and covered their words
under a tired hush
scoured by sand and seashells.
Then, near moonrise,
yawning and half-asleep,
they walked through the rising smoke
of leaves and pine cones,
the watchfires of the village,
and made the past their hermitage.

And me too,
I wanted to fade out
like the thin wash of blue
misting over a far horizon,
speak in unison with the chorus
of sunset sounds
drifting in with the tide,

maybe tell in a notebook
sewn from wet leaves
my search for the imprint of their sandals:
the moon in yellow scallops
on the ruffled bay,
meeting history in the orange light
still flickering inside every shrine.

But now the sun coughs,
bending over a row of restaurants,
and bumps its head against an automobile.
A road cuts a mountain in half,
clouds drip with a new rain
that stings the skin of my arm,
and factories burn the sky every day.

You two old men,
faces shriveled and grooved
like the hills,
come back.
Step out of the smoke this time.
I've seen you almost every night,
dusted with ash from my campfire,
cracking lice on a thumbnail,
huddling over my shoulder
while I look up the names
of mountains and rivers in my guidebook,
then fading with the curl of blue
twisting from a last ember.
Come back.
Sit with me.
Show me the meaning
of the slot in the sky
between a pair of hotels.
We have an hour before the fog rolls in.

A Restless Night
for Cynthia

The night surrounds me in a dark grey fog.
I feel its chill even under my *futon*.
The *tatami* underneath stiffens my spine.
I am tense and rise to snap on the light,
Set her photographs out before me on the floor.
I take out the old cardboard *hana* cards
My grandfather gave me and pretend she is here
To play this game of old men and young lovers.

The cards show me prints of the wooden sailboat
Piled up to its masts with cherry blossoms.
Young Prince Genji dips his umbrella
To acknowledge the small orange frog
Playing among pine boughs by the river.
The crane of a thousand days
Considers the swollen red sun of dusk.
Brown ducks fly in a triad over a charred field.

I deal the cards first to her picture,
Smiling as a breeze ruffles through her long hair.
I draw the full moon into my hand
And we go through the plays quickly.
The animal pictures come to me:
A golden-haired yearling buck, butterflies
Flickering around a cluster of peonies.
She takes the red rice bowl, chrysanthemums,
Green stalks of rice plants, and maple leaves
Blazing like filaments of dawn in a basket.

The game is over too soon.
I feel the chill of night
Clench into a fine mist,
Low on the ground outside.
At my window, I see the stars go out.
I pour myself a cup of wine.
Alone again, I drink with the moon.

Roots

There are seven steps to heaven,
and enlightenment stares me in the face
every morning when I shave.

I know this much because
I've walked up and down the spine of my soul,
searching for a name in the country
my ancestors had called their own.
Every mountain was a shrine there,
and had spires of cindercone pine
that could snag a cloud or crane,
and bring it down to the human throat
in a throb of religious song.
I learned there was a signature to all things
the same as my own, and that my own sight
sanctified streetlights and stalled cars
the same as ceremonies in solitude.

When I came back to California,
to the foothills stubbled with wild oat
and valleys ragged with housing tracts,
I appreciated the joy of street slang and jive,
the thrill of girl-watching
without guilt or conniving,
and sensed I had come to own my face
in whatever state or prefecture,
in whatever place.

II.

These days an old man hangs over my sleep,
mumbling behind a screen of dreams,

painting a landscape of sandspits,
fishing shacks, and terraced hills
struggling for space on a wave-hewn coast.
He walks on the sound of a snore,
the renegade sage and sorcerer,
laughing and laughing from his place
in the corner of that scroll.
It is his signature that scratches
across my unconscious life,
that leaves the luminous stamp of the moon
on every month of my memory.
It is for him I take the *shakuhachi*
to the desert's dead shore
and conjure up a melody of bamboo reeds,
cryptomeria, or blue lotus flowers
from the pastel silences of Mojave sage and lupine.
It is for him I learn a buffalo dance,
step out the trace of a dry wash,
and speak the grammar of a trance.
So now I study spells in Sanskrit
and memorize a tenor sax lick,
knowing my Self to be my faith,
my life to be my mate.

One day soon, the old man and I
will go off together toward the Sierra,
squat on the brow of a sculptured hill,
tip the cup of sky to our lips,
drink a *saké* of cactus juice,
and wait for the moon to rise
over the salt flats near Manzanar.

And so, my sutra comes around midnight,
and I chant it to the tune of "A Love Supreme":

MAKA HANYA HARAMITA SHIN GYO
A LOVE SUPREME
A LOVE SUPREME
SUPREME, SUPREME
A LOVE SUPREME
GYA TE GYA TE
HA RA GYA TE
HARA SO GYA TE
SOWA KA
HAN NYA SHIN GYO

When I pace the seven steps of the shrine in my soul,
the old man of my dreams will be me,
leaning into the wind blowing off the Mojave,
over Sierra passes and stands of sequoia,
circling around L.A. to spin out past Catalina
across the Pacific all the way to Asia,
and heritage will be an ancient flute
throbbing from its place in my heart
where his heart has found its roots.

1

Go out to the bridge over the river.
Is it the Sacramento?
It doesn't matter.
Go out there anyway.
The noises you hear
are the footsteps
of a thousand families
raining on the planks
of the bridge.
They run from something.
They wear heavy clothes,
carry bundles of kitchenware,
a jewel box, maybe some blankets
wrapped in huge purple
and scarlet pillowcases.

But they are not
pillowcases. I only
tell you that because
you might not understand
if I said *furoshiki*,
a green one the color
of freshly picked bracken.

The people continue to run.
It is February and rainclouds
thicken over the blue oaks
and bristlegrass in the valley.
A wind from the Bay, coming up
the deltas from offshore Japanese Currents,
rinses through buckeye and loquat trees,

rinses through dirt farmroads,
and plumes the wake of a pickup
hurtling down the foothills beyond.

No one carries food.

A mother dressed in evening clothes:
a long black gown, the flat-topped
round hat like a pillbox with its grey
veil of camouflage draped over her face,
her mouth like crushed rose petals
fresh with the shock of lipstick
(she could be going to a cocktail party);
carries an infant girl in her arms
like a sack of groceries
and picks her way through the crowd,
the white fin of a baggage tag
pinwheeling like a kite on her breast.

2

We knew only that the Exclusion Act
of 1882 did not admit Chinese women
unless already married to a shopkeeper,
did not allow men without fathers
already mining or blasting a path
through the gold mountains of California,
did not sanction the mix of races,
the miscegenation of yellow with white.

After all the veins had collapsed
from the needles of a thousand mine shafts,
after all the rail was laid
and the last spike driven through,
the laborers were collected in cattle pens
and then chased back home to Frisco

or shipped to Kwantung across the sea.
If they refused to be herded,
they were buried where they stood.

Those who survived learned the tricks
of forgery and invented sons
they never had, claimed cousins
in the villages back home
as brothers, and smuggled wives
and sisters through the Golden Gate.
They sang the songs of wild geese,
tried their luck in the fan-tan
and mah-jongg parlors of Chinatown,
shipped produce, stocked bitter melon
and chicken claws in big glass jars,
laundered the shirts, pressed the pants,
and sent their checks
to Charles Crocker's National Bank.

And, like winter chrysanthemums,
they flourished.

We knew from the Anti-Alien Land Law
of 1913, from the Exclusion Act of 1921,
that our Issei grandfathers could not
own land or claim citizenship.
So the lands were leased, rented,
or else bought and registered
in the names of their children
who were native-born
and therefore citizens.

Moses Tadao Miura, the deeds said.
Rachel Sawako Honda, said another.

And the Issei, the first generation,
went on with the planting, the harvest,
while machetes probed through the streets
pulling a few sailors by the hand,
and the vectors of a thousand war planes,
like swarms of huge dragonflies,
cut across Hawaiian skies.

3

Why do you ignore us?
We give you songs of grief
and you run to the liars
who would have you believe
that the past
is to laugh at,
its lesson best told
in a fairy tale
about the Nisei
emerging full-grown
Americans at birth,
leaping from the pit
of a huge peach
the Issei found
tumbling along a dry wash
in the River of Angels.

This is a lie.
Our history is bitter:
a farmer's thick arm
slashed on the spiked teeth
of barbed-wire fences,
a woman raising children
on spoonfuls of tumbleweed
and wrapping her feet in burlap
as she goes out to work the fields.
It is José

losing a leg
hopping the Santa Fe,
a hotel room,
one plate, one spoon,
and no woman.
It is someone's son
writing letters home
(home to Camp in Poston,
Minidoka or Jerome)
from the grey deck of a troopship
grumbling towards the real war,
where Anzio waits under shrouds
of fog and camouflage
to break his body
into a patchwork
of red blossoms.

This is not beautiful, you say.
This is not what we came for.
But who knows this better
than your grandfather
who spent the years
of his internment
sealed in the adobes
at Leuppe in Arizona,
sleeping on packed earth floors
under sheepskin blankets,
and twisting the iron bars
of his cell, until that day
in '45 when they told him
Hiroshima was nothing
but gas and scattered ashes
and black rain falling
and still falling
from the skies?

Why do you give me fairy tales?

Fairy tales are for children.

I am your stepchild.

Tell me,
your one bastard,
tell me the truth.

4

What I know—
the handful of stories,
brief chronologies
and photocopies of documents—
doesn't come from schools
or even the few infrequent
gatherings of the family.
It's not talked about.
Not shared.
Something stopped the telling.
Someone pulled out the tongues
of every Nisei
raped by the felons
of Relocation.

But there are records
and newspapers to read through,
at least a hundred years of them,
and letters and diaries
in the two languages.

There are generations,
four of them, documented
in newsprint with genealogies,

obituaries, births, driver's licenses,
land sales, moving sales, leases,
and "Evacuation! Must Sell!" sales.

Now I read
both halves of the history,
the before and the after,
the English and the Japanese—

> On the old railroads,
> the jobs they gave to Japanese
> were mainly cleaning the engine
> or else stupid chores in the roundhouse.
> Important mechanics were all whites.
> We worked eleven hours a day
> and had one hour for lunch.
> We lived in old freight cars
> lined up on a siding
> beside the roundhouse,
> away from any people.
> White people, I mean.
> There was always at least six of us
> in every car. The bunks were wooden
> rack beds spread with straw,
> blankets and bedding over that.
> Nobody used white sheets.
>
> (Tokio Akagi)

> In the coal mines around Rock Springs,
> there were more than ten thousand miners,
> but only two hundred were Japanese.

> My father told me that from 1906 to 1912
> there had been more than two thousand.
> On the Emperor's Birthday, to celebrate,
> they dressed up in armor and helmets,

paraded in the city like warriors.
Even in my day there were two pool halls
just for Japanese, two pro photographers,
grocery and fish stores, a noodle shop
and even a fancy restaurant folks went to
on payday. After the War, I went to visit
my father's grave at Rock Springs,
and for the first time I noticed
there were hundreds of tombstones,
young people in their twenties,
the victims of coal mine accidents.
　　　　　　　　　　(Paul Chikamasa Horiuchi)

5

Out of this only ten or twelve books,
a handful:

> *Issei*
> 　*Aiiieeeee!*　　*China Men*
> 　　　*No-No Boy*
> *Years of Infamy*
> 　*Before the War*
> 　　　*Eat a Bowl of Tea*
> *You Lovely People*
> 　*All I Asking for Is My Body*
> 　　　*Yokohama, California*
> *Hawaii: End of the Rainbow*
> 　*Longtime Californ'*
> 　　　*America Is in the Heart.*

Where are the histories,
our tragedies, our books
of fact and fiction?

Where are the legends,
the Iron Moonhunters
smudging the skies of Wyoming

with black dragonsmoke,
the Buddha Bandits
tumbling out of the Sierra
and raiding along the San Joaquin,
the *manongs* rising from a pumpkin field
painting the ground, the vines,
the flowers, and all the fruits blue?

Where are the myths, the tales?

> *It was autumn,*
> *the season for planting cauliflower.*
> *I went to the field at six in the morning*
> *and worked until six in the afternoon.*
> *I followed a wagon that carried*
> *cauliflower seedlings. The driver*
> *stopped now and then to drop a handful*
> *of the seedlings between the long furrows.*
> *I picked up the seedlings with one hand*
> *and dug into the ground with the other;*
> *then, putting a seedling into the hole,*
> *I moved on and dug another hole.*
> *I could hardly move when six o'clock came.*
> *I climbed into the wagon*
> *that took me slowly to the town.*
>
> (Carlos Bulosan)

They are with the poets,
the scholar transcribing
talks with survivors,
the masters of the stage,
the novelists collecting cosmologies
and spinning out their prophecies
on long, loose-rolled scrolls
of red and black ink.

They are with your grandmother
and mine, locked in photographs
curling with age, starting to fog
in their black lacquer boxes.

Where are the blessings?

> *I learned that the Filipino dishwasher*
> *at the Opal Cafe had died of poisonous*
> *mushrooms which he had picked somewhere*
> *in the valley. I took his place. It was*
> *notorious for its Saturday night crowd.*
> *Some two hundred school boys and girls*
> *came for refreshments and sandwiches*
> *after the dance at the auditorium.*
> *Because they came only when the cook*
> *was gone, I did all the work in the kitchen.*
> *It was a new experience. When I was rushing*
> *the orders, some of the boys brought*
> *their girls into the dark side*
> *of the kitchen and made love to them.*
> *I cursed them under my breath, made*
> *the sandwiches and spat on the bread.*
> *They were always drunk and careless*
> *with foul words, shoving a bottle*
> *of whiskey into my mouth, and laughing*
> *when the tears came. . . .*
>
> (Bulosan)

They are in the slice
of a bolo knife
cutting through cane,
cutting the throats
of a million salmon.

6

The Dragon wants me to scream,
to swear at my father
for burying anger
in the red dirt
beside the freckled aloe plants,
curse my mother
for salving a lifetime of pain
in the balm
of a loving house.

The Shark wants me to kill,
to tear at the throats
of white children,
exterminate them
like the Angels of Auschwitz.

But my wife,
a descendant of Mennonites
and Quakers
who nursed the sick
at Manzanar,
who comforted the crying
at Gila River,
who rowed the long boats
of their outrage, their protest,
into the shoal of storms
gathering on the peaks
of Heart Mountain,
is white.

There is always a need
to hate, a need to find
victims for that hatred.

Revenge blisters my tongue,
works in these words, says,
"Teach a Blessingway."

The Shark is a necklace
of teeth, pearls of blood
roped around my throat.

The Dragon is smoke
curling from prayersticks
around my campfire.

7

Lately, this past winter,
on the warm days
when the sun shuffles
unsashed with clouds
across the blue stone of sky,
I take my books and tablets,
my pens and small radio
with its sharp rasp of a voice,
and sit out in the living room
in just my shorts,
lie on the big front sofa
under the louvered windows,
try to catch the light
and chant a song
to the opening day.

I listen as the beach
sighs and shrugs its shoulders
under a long blue work-shirt
of surf; I think about Greece,
Spain, or Catalina across the Channel,
the island's rocky hillsides
slate grey through the haze.

I think about the kid
out in the driveway below,
tinkering with the choke,
adjusting the clutch,
oiling the long whips
of brake cables
on his big Harley bike.

I think about nothing
for a change, think
what it is that flowers
from itself and shakes
the yellow dust of thought
onto the red cloisters
of my heart, my passions.

And the sun blonds nothing
but the sands outside my window
and melons ripening on the sill,
the yellow ones we call bitter.

Issei:
First-Generation Japanese American

An old man turning pages of books
Left to right. He reads backwards,
Up and down, *kanji* and *kana* script,
Over and over again. He does not see
The old words any more. The meanings
Lost, he pauses on a page and curls
His fingers, surrounding one lone
Character in the cradle of his hand.
He turns, knowing that I watch him
And pity the sleep in his eyes.
This is your name, he says,
We take it from son of prince.
Kaoru is your name.

The Hongo Store
29 Miles Volcano
Hilo, Hawaii
from a photograph

My parents felt those rumblings
Coming deep from the earth's belly,
Thudding like the bell of the Buddhist Church.
Tremors in the ground swayed the bathinette
Where I lay squalling in soapy water.

My mother carried me around the house,
Back through the orchids, ferns, and plumeria
Of that greenhouse world behind the store,
And jumped between gas pumps into the car.

My father gave it the gun
And said, "Be quiet," as he searched
The frequencies, flipping for the right station
(The radio squealing more loudly than I could cry).

And then even the echoes stopped—
The only sound the Edsel's grinding
And the bark and crackle of radio news
Saying stay home or go to church.

"Dees time she no blow!"
My father said, driving back
Over the red ash covering the road.
"I worried she went go for broke already!"

So in this print the size of a matchbook,
The dark skinny man, shirtless and grinning,
A toothpick in the corner of his smile,
Lifts a naked baby above his head—
Behind him the plate glass of the store only cracked.

C & H Sugar Strike
Kahuku, 1923

You waken to food,
hot yellow tea on cold rice,
a dash of *shoyu*,
Louisiana Red,
a few tangles of *daikon*

glistening like angel
hair in the *chazuke* bowl.
You waken to a
new wife, humming jazz
tunes over the kitchen sink,

rinsing radishes
as she coaxes water out
of the iron pump.
You waken to the
old worries, shining like loose

change in a church plate,
tears of light beading under
gas lamps while the hymns
rummage through shallow
pockets, and the memories

flicker into bloom
with the dawnlight bleeding through
porch screens into the
kitchen, where it falls
at your feet like scattered rice.

A drift of incense
migrates from over the hills
    behind the village
    of Quonset barracks,
rinses through the dirt side streets,

    reaches the table
and settles into your hands
    where you read it like
    a message: The burn
has started. The strike is killed.

Kubota

In the back room of the plantation store,
Kubota drinks a strong Puerto Rican rum,
chases it with the dried flesh of cuttlefish,
and sings an old song he learned
in a cardroom back in Hiroshima.

He sings purple wine and red plum blossoms,
blossoms skittering in the rough wind
from off the Sea of Japan,
blossoms that swirl like snowflakes
falling on the soft muzzles of deer
grazing under willow trees in the public park.

He corks the last bottle,
slides it on the shelf
behind the pistols and ammo,
and steps out into the warm cloak
of a tropical night in Laie.

He laughs and lights a cigarette,
breathes out a wreath of smoke
for his funeral, fifty years away,
scents the air with the acrid incense of tobacco,
and blesses the wind that will scatter his ashes.

And Your Soul Shall Dance

for Wakako Yamauchi

Walking to school beside fields
of tomatoes and summer squash,
alone and humming a Japanese love song,
you've concealed a copy of *Photoplay*
between your algebra and English texts.
Your knee socks, saddle shoes, plaid dress,
and blouse, long-sleeved and white
with ruffles down the front,
come from a Sears catalogue
and neatly complement your new Toni curls.
All of this sets you apart from the landscape:
flat valley grooved with irrigation ditches,
a tractor grinding through alkaline earth,
the short stands of windbreak eucalyptus
shuttering the desert wind
from a small cluster of wooden shacks
where your mother hangs the wash.
You want to go somewhere.
Somewhere far away from all the dust
and sorting machines and acres of lettuce.
Someplace where you might be kissed
by someone with smooth, artistic hands.
When you turn into the schoolyard,
the flagpole gleams like a knife blade in the sun,
and classmates scatter like chickens,
shooed by the storm brooding on your horizon.

Dream of a Trumpet

I've been dreaming
of an orange trumpet
that shines through its wrappings
of velvet cloth,
that smells of polish and whale oil
as its brass keys
pump up and down,
lazily, like carousel ponies
in a carnival
stopped for the night
in my neighborhood park.
Calliope music mingles,
swirls with the surflike thrash
of freeways not far off,
and I can make out
the hissing of compressors
and the deep, hydraulic
grind of a Ferris wheel
turning slowly in its orbit
around my sleep.
All this and gaudy constellations
of neon and old Christmas lights
strung through dime-pitch booths,
the shooting gallery, and Pepsi stand,
echoes an embroidery of lilies,
pale blue and white,
on the *kimono* my mother wears
as she dances in a slow circle
around the fair and its crowd.
She holds her fan up.
It blooms like a flower
on the long stalk of her arm
and she gestures
with a toss of her head

towards paper lanterns
pitching in a light breeze
along the eaves of the church
that has just appeared.
Suddenly, I know
it is *Bon-Odori,*
the Festival for the Dead,
and half of Gardena
is dancing in the four streets
around the Buddhist Temple,
and the music I hear
is an old swing band
playing showtunes and *ondos* from Japan.
The trumpet blares,
and I can tell
that the man who plays it
will never care
whether the notes he makes
will survive him
or scatter in fragments of light
splashing across my face
as I turn in my sleep
and grumble something almost audible.

On the Last Performance of **Musumé Dojoji** at the Nippon-Kan of the Astor Hotel, Seattle, Washington

Something still remains
from the fall of '41,
in the theater of the Astor Hotel,
behind its windows shuttered with planking.
It's in the floorboards,
in the stack of old programs
yellowing in the sanctuary
of a backstage dressing room,
and a photograph of the cast
curled and peeling loose from its paper.
The bouquet of mauve and violet chrysanthemums
the thin butcher brought for the girl
who danced the legend of *Musumé Dojoji*
and which she forgot on the mirror-stand
beside an open tray of greasepaint
has withered and turned
to a handful of blue powder
drifting and about to scatter
in the draft
from the opened stage door.

When he enters, picking his way
past the pile of broken chairs
stacked under the balcony's overhang,
he lights a match and makes a lantern
with the cupped shrine of his hands
and guides himself by the flare
of its yellow light.
Dust devils bloom under his shoes,
roll away in a chorus of shadows
that swirl into life,
die into nothing
as he approaches the stage.

He hums something from Brahms,
or maybe a tune he picked up
in a piano bar on King Street,
late at night, drinking *saké* with friends
after the Festival for the Dead,
and it's better now because
he's gotten up the steps downstage,
stands facing the cinder-block wall
scarred with an arcana of names,
dates, fugitive and hostile messages
that no one cared to erase.

This is okay, he says to himself,
this doesn't mean any more
than MIMOSA IZUMI—1938,
than SANFORD HAYASE KISSES ASS,
than JAPTOWN IS MY TOWN CHINA STAY OUT;
and the dead don't mind
that he's never washed a gravestone
or left flowers or lit incense
and paid for a priest to chant
when it might have mattered.

A flute whistles, someone's hand
slaps at the tuned hide of a *kotsuzumi*,
and voices strum through the walls
in the harmonies of a new adagio
rolling out from everything he never knew
of the past and all its privacy.

She glides on slippers of blue silk,
stepping from behind the flag of damask
that curtains the theater's far wing.
Her hair trails behind her,
spilling over the white blaze of her neck
and down the folds of her robe

in a long tangle across the stage.
Something howls in his throat,
choirs like memory, as she snakes
out of her gown
and stands before him, naked
as the match flame flickering out
under the warm breath of a word.

Something Whispered in the Shakuhachi

No one knew the secret of my flutes,
and I laugh now
because some said
I was enlightened.
But the truth is
I'm only a gardener
who before the War
was a dirt farmer and learned
how to grow the bamboo
in ditches next to the fields,
how to leave things alone
and let the silt build up
until it was deep enough to stink
bad as night soil, bad
as the long, witch-grey
hair of a ghost.

No secret in that.

My land was no good, rocky,
and so dry I had to sneak
water from the whites,
hacksaw the locks off the chutes at night,
and blame Mexicans, Filipinos,
or else some wicked spirit
of a migrant, murdered in his sleep
by sheriffs and wanting revenge.
Even though they never believed me,
it didn't matter—no witnesses,
and my land was never thick with rice,
only the bamboo
growing lush as old melodies
and whispering like brush strokes
against the fine scroll of wind.

I found some string in the shed
or else took a few stalks
and stripped off their skins,
wove the fibers, the floss,
into cords I could bind
around the feet, ankles, and throats
of only the best bamboos.
I used an ice pick for an awl,
a fish knife to carve finger holes,
and a scythe to shape the mouthpiece.

I had my flutes.

*

When the War came,
I told myself I lost nothing.

My land, which was barren,
was not actually mine but leased
(we could not own property)
and the shacks didn't matter.

What did were the power lines nearby
and that sabotage was suspected.

What mattered to me
were the flutes I burned
in a small fire
by the bath house.

*

All through Relocation,
in the desert where they put us,
at night when the stars talked
and the sky came down
and drummed against the mesas,
I could hear my flutes
wail like fists of wind
whistling through the barracks.
I came out of Camp,
a blanket slung over my shoulder,
found land next to this swamp,
planted strawberries and beanplants,
planted the dwarf pines and tended them,
got rich enough to quit
and leave things alone,
let the ditches clog with silt again
and the bamboo grow thick as history.

*

So, when it's bad now,
when I can't remember what's lost
and all I have for the world to take
means nothing,
I go out back of the greenhouse
at the far end of my land
where the grasses go wild
and the arroyos come up
with cat's-claw and giant dahlias,
where the children of my neighbors
consult with the wise heads
of sunflowers, huge against the sky,
where the rivers of weather
and the charred ghosts of old melodies

converge to flood my land
and sustain the one thicket
of memory that calls for me
to come and sit
among the tall canes
and shape full-throated songs
out of wind, out of bamboo,
out of a voice
that only whispers.